The Mask Behind the Mask

The Mask Behind the Mask

Shana W. Gourdine

Library of Congress Control Number: 2019902154

ISBN:	Hardcover	978-1-7960-1764-9
	Softcover	978-1-7960-1763-2
	eBook	978-1-7960-1768-7

Print information available on the last page.

Rev. date: 02/22/2019

To order additional copies of this book, contact:
Xlibris
1-888-795-4274
www.Xlibris.com
Orders@Xlibris.com
788147

CONTENTS

This book is to everyone who helped mold me
into this phenomenal woman I am today.
To my beautiful daughters, Leonna M. Gourdine-Walker and Samria E. Gourdine-Walker.
To the love of my life, for always pushing me to be greater than before. You always told me I can do great things. Thank you for pushing me to be a star.
To my mother, my hero. She encouraged me to always work hard and follow my dreams and taught me how to be strong through the hard times.
To my father, who always pushed me to have faith and the courage to do anything.
To my siblings, who always encouraged me to be the best example of myself I can be.
To my second mom, who always spiritually encouraged me to have faith to God, who guides and protects me wherever I go.
To my sister circle of love, which helped mold me into the motivated, strong, and powerful queen I am.
Thanks to all my friends and family who have helped and supported me through this journey.

Introduction

Shana

Born to show the power of compassion and sympathy toward others, a person with a heart of gold and a lending hand. Even when she has nothing left for herself, she will put the needs of others before hers. She cares for all, disregarding their statuses or backgrounds. Her generosity and kindness know no bounds.

This book is to motivate you to look behind the mask and know that it is okay to cry, to be sad, to be mad, and to love who you are through it all.

We all wear masks, but there is always a mask that we still hide behind, always another face that we hide behind so that others don't see us. Just know that it is okay to love all of yourself, including the faces you try to hide behind.

Warrior of Many Strengths

I am a warrior beyond measure. Life is an uphill battle. It can be a very triumphant battle of storms. We need to make a stand to fight through the process. Different shortcomings in life can cause you to want give up or make you want to turn to other avenues. Stand tall and don't allow the devil to interrupt your process of glory. With God's grace and mercy, I will continue to push through pain, sickness, mental struggles, emotional feelings, battles with chronic illness. God has me until the end of time. Many of us want support and need the support as we transform and undergo better healing. As I take my stand in my triumphant battles of health, I will stand and walk with faith and strength through Jesus. *I am a warrior of many strengths.*

Overcomer

I am an overcomer of my situation despite the emotional, physical, and mental abuse that I endure. **You have to learn to remove yourself from your situation to** reach a **successful position.** You have to want to have joy, peace, and happiness. **I overcame my situation and took the path of** happiness. My soul was hungry to fight to get back to being normal. We could not depend on being scared, hurt, depressed, or lost and let devil win. That was not an option. With God's grace and mercy, I found my strength to step out and counter my fear. **In order to** overcome, you have to fight. You have the ambition and the drive to not let your situation make the final decision in your life. Say out loud, "I am an overcomer." Be determined.

Wishing

As I sit here, thinking of the smell of your cologne,
As I sit here, thinking of the way you walk and talk,
As I sit here, thinking of the dos and don'ts,
Wishing and wondering, "Is this a joke?"
As I sit here, thinking that you are amazing and charming,
As I sit here, thinking that you are caring and loving,
Wishing and wondering, "Is this real or an imitation in the sky?"
All I want is love, care, honesty, loyalty, respect, and
to be treated like gold (queen of your world).
As I sit here, thinking if you are the one
who is going to make me whole,
Wishing you are the man to make me twirl,
Then there is no more wishing, wondering,
because you're the one I adore.

Courage

When you think about courage, you see someone as being a hero.

Well, today, you can be your own hero.
Be your own strength. Be your own savior.
Be your own advocate to fight for your life.
Courage is to be able to soar above your situation.
Despite the struggles, keep being in courage to become a better you.

As you walk through the journey, be encouraged
by a quote, a motivation speech,
Words, songs, and poems,
Whatever makes you encouraged to fight another day.
Encourage yourself to love yourself first.
No one else is going to be a better advocate than you for yourself.
Always know that God is there as you be your
hero, as you walk through this journey.

I Am

I am a counter.
I am an overcomer.
I am a warrior.
With strength, hope, and courage, you can become all these things.
Master of life, give us difficult tasks to overcome to
counter the situation or even be warriors through it.
Despite the situation or the struggle at hand, we have to fight.
We have to fight to be happy.
We have to fight to be strong.
We have to fight to have joy.
We have to be greater than our situations.
There are moments when you have you will say, "*I can't do this.*
I'm not going to make it. I don't want to be here. Why me?"
These are the questions of life's purpose we ask ourselves.

This is when you dig deep down inside of you to
find that warrior who is ready for battle.
Just say, "*I am!*"
Despite what anyone says, thinks, or feels, you need to know that
You are a counter.
You are an overcomer.
You are a warrior.
"*I am somebody!*"

Look at Me

Look at me. Do you know?
What image do you see?
Look at me.
What judgment do you have of me?
Look at me.
What gossip do you have about me?
Look at me.
What harsh things do you have to say?

When you look back at yourself, what do you to say about yourself? When you ponder on your life and everyday struggles, how do you judge yourself? How do we evaluate ourselves in everyday living? Elevate yourself by loving yourself for who you are. Appreciate who you are, what you stand for. Don't allow anyone to change your character. Love yourself so much so that if they don't know how to treat you, you know your worth. Know what your values and morals are. Don't lower your standards because they are not evaluated to your level. Don't allow anyone to interrupt your piece. Stay motivated and focused.

Light Of

As you look into the sky, you see the light of hope.
As you walk outside, you feel the light of hope.
As you open your eyes, you see your journey of hope.
As you walk and breathe and take in life, you
are inspired to be greater than before.
As you become full with ambition, determination,
courage, you know that the light of hope is near.
Your inner strength will pull you through that hope of light to the
other side of your journey, where you know that everything is all right.

Smiling

When all else is failing, be able to smile through
the pain, the sorrow, the storm.
Smile because you know it is going be a brighter day.
Smile because you know it could be you who didn't
wake up. It could been you who is homeless with no
food. It could be you who can move out of bed.
Smile because you're standing. Smile because you're walking.
Smile because you're talking, hearing, and seeing.
Smiling can be an amazing thing.
Smile a little because it could change a person's day.
Smile because you are that amazing.

Power

I am powerful.
I have strength.
I have peace.
Everything that is positive, I am.
I am a person who won't take no for an answer.
If there is something I want, I am determined to get it.
Nothing can stop me as long as I walk with faith.

The power of wisdom, the power of courage, and the power of
strength, all combined, are the weapon for battle of the Savior.
All these things encourage you to be a powerful person.

Any path you take, there will be a hill to climb,
but to make that journey a little easier, have all the
power to be strong through your life travels.
Stay the course. There is a light at the end of your transformation.

Control

Always know your power.
We allow people to control our character.
We allow people to change our mood.
We give people too much control.
We shouldn't let people determine an hour, a
minute, or even a second of our day.
Minimize the amount of space you allow
people to occupy in your mind.
Don't allow anyone to upset you, to take you out of your character.

Always remember you are the only person
who controls how your day goes.
Stop letting the negative control your life and reach
for the positive in your life and let it lead.
Control your desire of your day. If you say it is
going to be a good day, let it be a good day.
You control your atmosphere!

Motivation

What motivates you to be better?
We want to be better for our friends.
We want to be better for our family.
We want to be better for world image.
When are you going to say, "I want to be better for me"?
The best motivation is to do it for yourself.
When you do things to please others, it will never give you victory.
You have to want it yourself to feel the empowerment.
Happiness comes from within oneself,
The motivation of one entire soul,
The sparkle that makes one smile at little things.
Always do things from your entire heart to get that soul motivation,
Makes you feel like you're soaring above all others.
Soar like an eagle!
Amazing.
All the walls are falling.
All the strength is removed from me.
All the courage is fading out of me.
All the wisdom is disappearing from me.

Lost

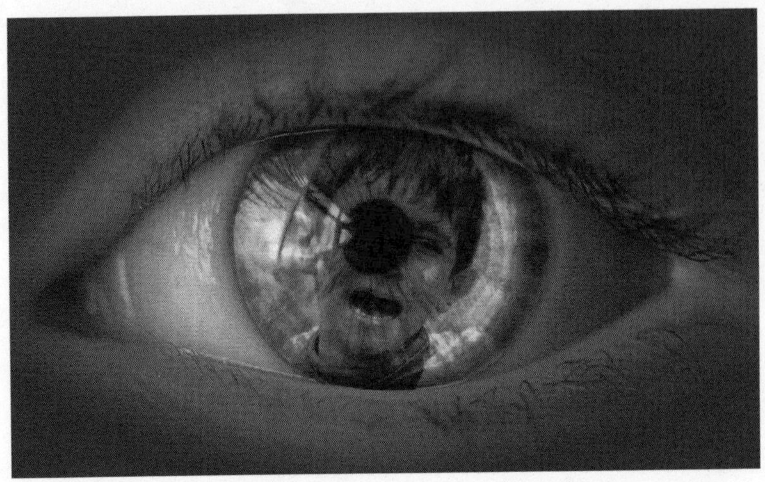

Have you ever felt so lost, very confused, and worried?
Have you ever felt so judged, very embarrassed, and filled with fear?
Let it stop, and stand tall with the warrior
strength you have inside of you.
Be amazing, dependent, and honest with yourself.
Allow yourself to be as heroic as the warrior inside of you.
Everyone has lost before. We have learn how to
overcome the darkness and live in the light.
Learn how to be amazing and stand in your glory.
Don't limit yourself from the greatness that
the Lord ordained for your life.
Don't fight what you call "maybe."
We all have a purpose to be here.
We all have to be ready to fight the battle that stands before us.
It is not always going to be good days. We need to know.
We are somebody.

When You

When you . . .
When you touch me,
My body gets weak.
When you kiss me,
My body starts to leak.
When you speak softly in my ears,
It makes me want to shed a tear.
When you look into my eyes,
All I want to do is stare.
When my thoughts of you are near,
They make me feel no fear.
When you leave me,
I want you near.
Holding you close to me,
I wish you never disappear.
The scent of you is so amazing.
It might make me want to let loose my hair.
Your body pressed next to mine
Makes me lose my mind.
When we are apart,
I have no fear because you are my dear.
Love is definitely in the air.

Without You!

Without me, there is no you.
Without you, there is no me.
Together we can make this a unity.
I cherish you as if you were a perfect fit, like a key.
I adore you as if you were a blessing sent from above.
I admire you as if you were a precious piece of jewelry.
Our souls are connected to make us a complete set.
Our love is a beautiful piece of art.
When I see you, I light up like a kid in a candy store.
When I hear your voice, I light up like a newborn baby.
I just want to take a moment to let you know
how much you mean to me.
Without you, there is no me!

Self-Love

Loving ourselves is the best thing we can do to ourselves. Never lower your standards to please others. At times, we allow people to make us feel less of a person. People try to play the victim, as if it is all our fault. Stand firm on how you feel. Don't allow anyone to make you feel less deserving. We sometime allow the people we love to treat us as less of a person, less of the value of what we are worth or deserve. Self-respect is where it starts. It starts inside you. If you don't respect yourself, people will get too comfortable. Stand for your self-respect. Stand for your self-worth, and *love yourself first.*

Love Soars

As love soars above the clouds,
I know you look down on me,
Casting down an armor of protection,
Sending all the love you have around.
As love soars above the sun,
I feel the presence of you all around.
Your memories are always and forever near.
I know you don't want us to shed a tear.
We will always keep you in our hearts.
I know that we are never really apart.
We know as love soars above the clouds, you are always looking down.

Love

Love is such a precious word,
A word that is filled with a lot of meaning,
A word that makes you think you're floating on air,
A word that has your heart fill with joy,
A word that can make you shed a tear.
Love is so special. It is the best,
A words that makes your body melt,
Can make your body shiver, even when you're not around.
Love is a word that brightens up your day when you're down,
Makes a rainy day into a sunny day.
Love is a word that you'll be happy to hear from
your special someone to show that they care.
Love is so precious. You need to know that
I love you and I care.
You're like my other soul that I feel when we are apart.
You are the other part that seems to
Keep me happy when I'm down.
You turn my frown into a smile.

Your sweet lips and your passionate kiss . . .
Is that what I miss?
Your sexy voice and just your perfect touch are never forgotten.
With you not being here right now,
I know we'll be together again.
It might seem long but never forever or eternity.
The longer I think, the quicker the days pass.
Missing you is now the past, but seeing you is soon the future.
So until then, I'll be missing you till the end.

Loving It

I love the smell of your body.
I dream of your touch.
When you make love to me, you make my body tremble.
When you take your time with your every stroke,
Lick me in every place that anyone can imagine,
Caress my body and hold me tight,
Love every moment of it so much, I want you to stay.
The night fulfills my every fantasy.
You made it a night I will never forget,
Licking me up and down my back,
Spreading my legs wide, waiting till you come inside,
Exploring every inch inside of me,
Exploring my world so deep inside me, making me squirm,
Making love to me until I say stop, or just
making my body rise to the top,
Loving every moment of it. We are going to lock
the door, and let's explore a little more.

Miracle

Are you a miracle? Are you that special one who was sent
from the Lord above? I know that I was looking for a special
someone to brighten up my life, to make me happy,
Also just makes me feel special because sometimes I can feel like
I was nothing or maybe I'm not pretty enough, but meeting you
Is just a miracle, to brighten up my day, to help
me out when I'm down or depressed,
To get me out of this stage of thinking that everyone is better than
me, The knowledge to know I am more than an average person.
Thank you for helping out. In the last two months, I have
felt like I am on top of the world. Now I have the confidence
that I can do anything and be anything I want.

Come In

Come in and close the door.
Take me to a world to explore,
A world of pure fantasy, not even thinking of any reality,
Taking my body to a world of lovemaking that can blow my mind.
Caress my body from head to toe while my
pussy starts to get dripping wet.
You stick your tongue so deep inside of me,
you might make me choke on it.
Loving every moment of my thoughts,
You look deep into my eyes,
kissing my lips, and start caressing my thigh and
are about to make my body explored,
Sliding your manhood inside me, making me
moan and groan, yell and beg for more.
Now you're inside. How did you enjoy the ride?

Satisfying You

I want to take you into a room, help you take off your clothes,
Lay you down on my bed,
Give you a nice massage from head to toe,
Caress your body front to back.
Let your imagination run wild so it will be a night you won't forget.
I start by making you comfortable.
As I touch and tease you and beg for me to please you,
As I look into your eyes, you're making me
come inside.
The pleasure that you are aiming for is what I adore.
That is why you are the one I was waiting for.
Now come inside. Let me see what I have in store.

Journey

As I walk through this journey of life, I feel one can't
imagine the pain I feel. No one can understand my
trails. No one can understand my depression.
As the phone rings, I hear your voice, and a smile comes
across my face. Everything about you brightens up my soul.
As your voice travels through the air waves,
you make my sadness disappear.
I never was sure if I could love again.
I never was sure if I could smile again.
As I wait for your call or text, you reassure
me that your love would never end.
As I continue on my journey of life, I know this joy will never end.

Eternity

Is this true?
Are you really my boo?
Is this a dream?
You are really catering to me.
Is this a movie?
You're truly treating me as a queen.
Is this a dream?
You're treating me as a star in my dream.
Is this a guarantee
That we can be together for eternity?

Emotions

With love, you come with a lot of emotions. They are a lot of laughs, smiles, and special moments. With every moment, the feelings you have for the person get stronger. You start to want to see their beautiful face and feel their delicate hands and want to enjoy their presence even more. You want to spend every waking moment with them. As these feelings arise in you, then question, "Is it lust, or can it be I am falling in love?" A lot of fear comes with the risk of commitment, the fear of being with one person when there is so much temptation in the world. As we continue on this roller coaster, we may get lost in a fantasy world. Some of us lose ourselves, who we are, because we are loving that other person more than we love ourselves. We want to make our partners very happy in the pleasure world. Sometimes we have to take time out for yourselves so as not to lose our souls in the moment. Take care of your partner, but make sure you take of yourself as well. Make sure that person tells you that they love you. They are taking care of you as well. While this journey continues, there will be some unhappy and unlovable moments that we encounter: fights, arguments, heated discussions, and sometimes a little disrespect. In the end, we are not living as perfect people, and we do not live with perfect people. Love, happiness, and a good relationship take work. You have to be willing to laugh, cry, and be able to work all things out to make it work.

The Pain We Feel

After being hurt so many times, how do you love again? How do let down those walls that you put up to protect your hurt? How do you find those happy places where your smile was so innocent? How do you stop the tears from falling from the pain you endure? How do you trust again and know that person is real and true? Hurt can cause a person to shut down. Hurt causes a person to shut down. Hurt causes so many different emotions to arise. Hurt puts you into a space that many people are these days. It is at the point where you don't want to let anyone in. You don't want to let anyone get close to you. You don't let anyone next to your hurt. The lack of trust, the lack of security—everyone is an enemy. We need to step back and hit the reset button. Go back to the time in your life when you were so innocent, with no pain, no hurt, no disappointment, no fear of loving people, back to times when there were no worries.

Healing after a Broken Heart

Give it to God and let him heal you.
Time heals all pain in your heart.
Start loving yourself and move on.
Pray for God to heal your broken pieces.

Life Storm

In life, we go through a lot of disrespect that we shouldn't allow. What we shouldn't deal with is disrespect, and we shouldn't tolerate it. As time progresses, we allow a few things to slide and allow these things to continue without correcting people on how we should be treated. That's when people get comfortable and feel they can treat you any kind of way, say anything that they want, and address you as if you were less of a person. When we forget to value our worth or what we deserve, we let what we stand for or deserve go out the window. You know how you should be treated. You know what you deserve. Never sell yourself short regardless of who it may be. Stand firm for your respect. We allow negative drama in our lives when we don't set boundaries for how people should treat us, how people should address us with the utmost respect. We let people get comfortable, never set boundaries, which then invites mental, physical, and emotional abuse. It starts off with the small things, and then it escalates over time. You have to love yourself first, know your worth, and don't accept anything less than that. Protect yourself from the hurt that you will endure if you don't stop it at the door. You deserve to be treated like a queen. Treat yourself like you treat others. All it takes is the self-love that you give to yourself, and demand the same respect from everyone else. Love yourself first, even if no one else loves you. God loves you through the good and the bad. You are the one person who understands yourself first. There are times when others attempt to understand you, but reality is God and yourself will be the only ones who truly understand you deep down. You can hide behind the smiles or the laughter while you pretend everything is okay. You can only put on so many faces to keep up the mask. God knows all and sees all. Stay true to who you are. Love all of you, including the good and the bad. You won't have to carry so many faces except your own.

To Be

To be with me is a dream.
To be with me is a fantasy.
I'll never let you down or never play you for a clown.
You should cherish what you have.
You should cherish what you see
'Cause in your dream, I could only be a fantasy.

Time

The time has come and gone
for us to say our goodbyes.
We had our good times, and we had our bad times,
But through it all, we made it.
You are like the wind beneath my wings,
The star in my night sky that I can make a wish on.
Having you by my side, I hope you will never disappear.
You know you are my heart and soul that make my night turn into day.
But now we have to separate, and that is enough said.
Always remember that besides me, there is God.
Having him and believing in him, you can
make it through until the end.

It's You

The first moment I laid my eyes on you, I knew there was something there. It was the most magical moment that I had ever felt. A feeling that words can't explain, it is a feeling that I had never felt from anyone before. Night and day, I am wishing and wondering, "Are we going to be together forever? Is this going to last forever?" My heartbeat rises every time we are together. You make my palms sweat. You make me so happy that I never want to let you go. Every time we talk, you are next to me, holding me close, next to you, in your arms. When I'm down, you make me happy, but my main reason for writing this poem is to let you know that It's you who keeps my heart rolling. It's you who keeps my stomach twisting. It's you. Everything about you makes me scream, "*Oh baby!*" Baby, it's you who finally won my heart.

The Rose

This rose is for the fire in my heart that burns
for you every time I see your face.
Can't you feel my pain crying in my heart?
Don't you see tears in eyes? Don't you see me dying inside?
The lost time, the lost memories, the lost trust of our situation . . .
One moment, you made me feel as if I was the only
one. You made me feel that it could only be us.
You made me feel as if I was your world or I could be your only girl.
This is the rose that is going to help me dry my eyes. This
rose is the fire in my heart that burns for you every time.

As the light dims and the shadow of darkness goes over
my room, I light a candle to give the room a smell,
A smell that I remember every time I was with you.
I lay across my bed, thinking of no other,
Thinking of all the times we spent together, longing
for the days that passed, missing you so much.
Well, for now, I have to just daydream of moments when we were never
apart, remember all the love and affection we felt for each other.
As you can see, the rose represents me blooming
from the hurt and pain that I have endured.

Printed and bound by PG in the USA